GET YOUR HEAD IN THE GAME

Lance Davis

ACKNOWLEDGEMENTS

I would like to thank the many people who helped me achieve my goals and write this book.

Sharon Wood, Lantern Lane with Project Troops, Don Norton, James Bartlett, Judge Andrew Valdez, Joe Clifford, Aaron Gilmore, Jim Schermerhorn, Sean Olsen, Robert Bills, Dave and Randy Marchant, Manny Herrera, Russ Anderson, CJ Jenkins, Scott Mecham, Tommy Ponzio, Mike Saunders, Jeff Alvari, Spencer Westwood, Chris Mcgrail, Jeremy Horn, Jake Heun, David Castillo, Amir Killah, Kerstin Martineau, Blake Myrick, Erik Rapp, Terry Putman, Gus Restwich, Raquel Comstock, Brad Tripp, Jody Tripp, Mike Haynes, Hedy Miller, Kevin Nieznanski, Carl Wimmer, Tim Prince, Joseph Dianacin, Justin Clifford, Sarah Tal, David Edgell, Bill Mott, Kaleb Crafts, Eric Millburn, Darren Carr, Ed Acey, Bud Davis, Leslie Burke Hofheins, Ed Kinsey, Kyle Moosman, Dennis Shock, John Cunningham, Aaron Sampson, Brian Meilke, Chad Drecksell, Dave Edmonson, Jill Yamashita, Sean Aberman, DerekWashburn, Mike Cordova, Nick Lenhart, Ricky Reinhardt, Austin Oseguera. Graphic Girl Design - Sherry Mendoza

Members of Brutal Powerlifting
Jeremy Horn's Elite Performance
Utah Powerlifters
All others I haven't mentioned, there are so many people to thank.

Most of all I give thanks to God.

This book is dedicated to my son *Samson*

FOREWARD

This book is about your mind and your thoughts
and how to become a winner.
God did not put us here to lose, he gave us our most
valuable asset, our mind, and because it is God-
given, we are all born winners.
The world has advanced, and incredible things have happened
since the beginning of time because of the power of the
mind. From the time man first took breath and
made a fire, to landing on the moon, things considered
impossible have happened again and again because of the
miracle gift of the mind.
Use your mind and reach heights you never considered. Make
your dreams come true.
No matter what level of life you currently occupy
you can improve, you can change, and you can
overcome. Everything is done through the power
of the mind. The mind helps you become a better
athlete, academic, business-person, or being of any
character and can make you a champion in all
aspects of life.
Champions in sports and every other area
of life do it by employing thinking to
control actions. There is a saying that to
reach a goal you must conceive it and
believe it, then achieve it.
This is as truthful as the sky is blue.
Believe in yourself.
You deserve to excel as much as anyone. We all
have it deep within our souls, but we must program
ourselves to do it.
Remember, your thoughts will make or break you.

CHAPTERS

·CHAPTER ONE·

YOUR MIND

Your mind, consciously or subconsciously controls everything you do. The mind controls and determines your success in everything from tying your shoes to breaking a world record in the Olympics. It is the controller of your life and your destiny. All emotions, actions, decisions and outcome of your life are related to your mind. If you want to be successful or if you want to be a champion, you need your mind to work for you and not against you. Your thoughts will make or break you, and the person who is controlling those thoughts is you.

Do not let negative people, thoughts, or words destroy you. Positive people, thoughts, and words will take you to places you have never been. We were born to be champions, and the mind is our compass. The principles taught in this book reveal how to use your mind to achieve athletic prominence. It doesn't matter your background, your genetics, or your circumstances. You are capable of realizing your goals, and of achieving greatness; but, you must believe and you must use your mind in order to properly pursue both.

The power of one's mind cannot be overemphasized. Remember that every achievement man has ever made came first from the mind. The mind controls the body, and we still do not know of what we are capable. In 1954, Roger Bannister first broke through the four minutes mile barrier He set a new world record of 3.98 for the first ever sub-four minute mile. Until that time, this feat was believed to be impossible. All the experts, scientists, doctors, and coaches said that a human being could not do this. It was believed that a human being would die before completing it because his lungs and heart would explode. It is not a coincidence that the target number was exactly four minutes. Many runners had recorded 4:01, 4:03, 4:05 anything but 4:00.

Similar beliefs had kept people from reaching similar milestones until someone else had shown the feat was achievable. Every athletic achievement that has stood for any inordinate length of time has because of the minds inability to believe it was possible to surpass. Two months after Bannister broke the mark John Landy, from Australia, also broke it. Many other runners broke it soon after that, and it has been done hundreds of times since. We must ask ourselves could the human body suddenly change enough that many runners were now were doing something that no one in history had done before?

The difference can only be in the mind. The world record now stands at 3:43 by Hicham El Guerrouj of Morocco. In fact in 1994 Eammont Coughlon of Ireland ran the mile in under four minutes when he was forty-one years old!

Until 1970, no Olympic weightlifter had ever completed a 500 pound clean and jerk. Many had tried, but no one could do it. Lifters had done 499.5, but no one could do 500. On September 20, 1970, Vasily Alexeev of the Soviet Union lifted 500 pounds, breaking the 500 pound barrier. Within two months, Serge Redding of Belgium and Ken Patera of the United States equaled Alexeeve's feat. The current world record is 580 pounds by Hossein Rezazazadeh of Iran setting it in 2004. Again, achieving the 500 pound clean and jerk, the human body could not have changed that much in a few months enabling others suddenly to be able to clean and jerk 500 lbs. These athletic milestones had never been a c h i e v e d in human history. It was in the mind.

Many consider Ed Coan to be the greatest powerlifter of all time. He deadlifted 901 pounds weighing in at the 220# class. He said the difference between a great and an average lifter was in the mind. He was a huge proponent of mindset to lift heavier weights.

On Good Friday, April 9, 1982, in Lawrenceville Georgia, Angela Cavallo's teenage son Tony was in the driveway working on a 1964 Chevy Impala. He had lifted it on a jack, removed a rear tire and was working on the suspension. Suddenly, Angela was alerted by a frantic knocking at her door. A neighbor shouted and told her there had been an accident in the driveway. She sprinted out the door to the driveway and found Tony trapped beneath the car. It had rocked off the jack and fallen with Tony beneath it. Although not immediately crushed, he was unconscious. Angela called for help; then she lifted the car enough that others were able to move Tony from danger. She saved her sons life by a seemingly impossible accomplishment.

You probably have heard similar stories. This one was verified through journalist Mariana Minaya. There was no way Angela Cavallo could lift a car, yet she did in order to save her son. Her mind told her she had to, and she did.

Prisoners of War have survived under conditions that should have killed them. Starvation, dehydration, and torture were used to control them. Some people have survived multiple gunshot wounds while others have died after being grazed by bullets. Why is this? It's the mind, it's your survival, it's your belief you can make it. If you get under the weight if you attempt a free throw or attempt a golf putt, your mind will make or break you. You are ready to squat, at the foul line, or standing over a putt, your adrenaline is pumping, and if you let your mind doubt even for a second, you will fail.

You must train your mind persistently. You are about to putt to win in a huge tournament. Every sound and movement around you must be oblivious to you. Every thought must be of the putt going in and nothing else. The slightest doubt and you will not make it. Does it sound hard to think this way? It is not. If you constantly train your mind to succeed, the thought of missing will not occur. The thought of failure will disappear. You will know in your heart you will beat your opponent, whether you are in the UFC or having a pick-up game of horse. Train your mind and your body will have no choice but to succeed. Like a robot under orders, your body will respond.

CHAPTER TWO·

YOUR SUBCONSCIOUS MIND

Your subconscious mind controls much of what you do without you knowing it. You need to learn to program your subconscious mind for success. Muscle memory is activated in your subconscious mind. Your subconscious mind makes thinking decisions and then your conscious mind reacts. For example: when you open a door, you immediately start to use the hand you have always opened it with. This is the subconscious mind in action. Try to open the door with the opposite hand, the one you are not used to. It's awkward. You have to make a conscious decision to open the door with the "wrong" hand. It follows that you must feed your subconscious mind with winning thoughts and experience to be successful.

This principle is noticeably true in athletic competition. You do not have time to consciously analyze every action you must take in order to be successful at a given moment. It must come from muscle memory and the subconscious mind. If your preparatory thoughts have been negative, you will have negative results. If you have prepared yourself with positive thoughts you will have positive results. Think about an outfielder breaking at the sound of the bat to be in the right place to catch the ball when it descends. Think about the defensive cornerback making the correct maneuvers on the run to intercept the pass. Think of a goalie's reaction to a projectile being kicked, hit, or hurled toward the net and how he must react to prevent a score. All are observable examples of positive practice and mental preparation resulting in positive results.

Everything the mind is exposed to goes into the subconscious mind and stays there. The subconscious is like a robot and cannot differentiate between reality and fiction. It merely reacts to what it receives. You must learn to control your subconscious mind. People overachieve and underachieve every day because of the contents of their subconscious. This phenomenon is not unique to sports. It is found in all aspects of life. Business, school, vocations, relationships, everything we do in all aspects of our lives, are controlled by our conscious or subconscious thoughts.

Dr. Joseph Murphy the author of the bestselling classic, "The Power of Your Subconscious Mind," said, among other statements, "There is only one process of healing, and that is faith. There is only one healing power namely your subconscious mind. Whether the object of your faith is factual or fabricated, you will get results. Your subconscious responds to the thought in your mind. Look upon faith as thought in your mind and that will suffice. Develop a definite plan for turning over your requests or desires to your subconscious mind. Great and noble thoughts on which you habitually dwell will become great acts." He also said "Watch your thoughts. Every thought accepted as true is sent by your brain to your solar plexus – your abdominal brain – and is brought into your world as reality." He also said, "Habit is the function of your subconscious mind." There is no greater evidence of the marvelous power of your subconscious than the force and sway habit plays in your life.

You are a creature of habit. Your habits will make a difference in you being a winner or not. You must become a slave to your habits as long as they are positive. Negative habits can destroy you, but good habits will turn you into someone you want to be. Develop respectable habits from your thought patterns and you will begin to do them without even thinking, as your subconscious takes over. Control your mind and you will win.

The most-effective way to control your subconscious mind is through hypnosis or hypnotherapy. If you want to improve your mental game and control your subconscious, practice hypnotherapy with a good hypnotherapist. You must also read material that will

help you to store success thoughts in your head. Chapter 3,

Train Your Mind, provides additional effective training methods.

Control your mind and you will control your body.

·CHAPTER THREE·

TRAIN YOUR MIND

T

rain your mind.

Why should you train your mind?

How should you train your mind?

The answer to the first question is because you MUST. All day, every day, your mind is subject to whatever you see, hear, read and think. If you don't learn to control this input, and take steps to train your mind and what to do with it, your mind will merely react to what it hears and sees which may spell disaster. Many people are unhappy and unmotivated because what they unconsciously subject their minds to is not positive. A large percentage of society is negative and most of what we see and hear each day in the media is also negative. That's why you must feed your mind with positive, uplifting, can-do material.

Mind training is similar to weight loss efforts. Most of us need to lose weight to be healthy and improve athletic performance. Just as you put the correct foods in your body to have a healthy body, you must put the correct thoughts in your mind to have a healthy mind. How do you feed your mind? You have to read and think positively and eliminate negative people, TV shows, movies and experiences from your life. You have to eliminate negative self-talk. Remove

14

can't and cannot rom your vocabulary. Eliminate the words afraid, timid and scared. All words have antonyms, words that have opposite meanings; and winners don't talk like losers. Sports hypnosis can be used to accomplish this, but you must go to a hypnotherapist who believes just as strongly as you do that you can be a champion. Substitute a self-help or motivational book instead of watching a meaningless TV show. If you do watch TV, find the channels with, constructive programming. Again, above all, use sports hypnosis. It works. Along with that, read a book that will stay in your mind and tell you that you can achieve your goals.

It's also important to read about the latest in training methods and strategies, diet and nutrition, and anything else that helps you get an edge on your opponent. Don't just workout and then watch TV all night or go goof off somewhere. Make time to read material that will improve your game. If you are an athlete, whatever your sport, there is a huge amount of research you can read to improve your game. Sadly in this day and age many people use our advanced technology for negative endeavors. Don't do this. You won't become a champion by constantly surfing the internet looking for immoral purposes or other meaningless endeavors.

15

Expand your mind. At the top levels of competition, you must get up on your competitors. In his best-known speech, Notre Dame Football Coach, Vince Lombardi, said you have to be smart to be number one in any business. This is true. Someone with less talent than you can beat you if they out work or out think you. Feed your mind. Once you achieve a winning mindset you will have desire and conviction you can do great things. If you fill your mind with the best information available, you can improve your will to excel. Seeking out the best coaches and trainers and asking them questions enables you to continue learning. You must never stop learning.

Surround yourself with people whose words and actions elevate you. Work on this every day from the moment you awaken until you drop off to sleep at night. Become a slave to the habit of thinking like a winner. Your body is controlled by your mind, not vice versa. Your subconscious mind will become flooded with winning thoughts and commands and will react. Without thinking, the subconscious will give results. You will see improvement in your game and how you feel. Train your mind.

·CHAPTER FOUR

VISUALIZATION

To excel in sports you need to visualize. You need to see yourself participating in your sport, both in practice and in competition. You must see yourself doing things the right way, with correct form and technique. You must see yourself being successful at whatever you are doing.

Setting short and long term goals enable you to see yourself achieving both. Watching athletes, especially golfers and powerlifters, is very revealing of how visualization works. When competitors have time to think about what they are about to do, attempt a lift or a putt, they tend to concentrate deeply, oblivious to what is going on around them. They may even close their eyes as they focus on their visualization of what they are about to do. They see themselves making the putt or successfully lifting the weight. If you see yourself making the putt or completing the lift, you increase your chances of successfully performing when it counts. You can use visualization anytime you are preparing for an event, and even when you are competing in sports that allow you to ponder what you are about to attempt, like throwing a pitch, shooting a free throw, lifting a weight, lining up a putt, etc.

Ken Patera the great Olympic weightlifter and strongman competitor from the United States used to sit in a room the day before the meet and visualize himself at the meet. He imagined the sights and sounds of the meet. He visualized every detail: getting ready, going to the platform, performing the lift, and returning the weight to the floor. Of course, his visualization was always of doing all of these things correctly and successfully completing them. He claimed he could gain an additional 10 to 15 pounds just by visualizing what he was going to do. If you're about to throw a pitch and you want to hit the inside corner for a strike, you better see it in your mind first. If you want to sink a free throw you better make it in your mind first. The more you practice and use visualization the better it works. If you have a basketball game tomorrow, you had better visualize yourself sinking every shot the night before.

Many athletes need to lose weight for competition. Wrestlers, boxers, Olympic weightlifters, power-lifters, MMA fighters, etc., often need to lose weight before competition. Sometimes they need to lose a lot of weight in a short time. Rarely do athletes exceed weight requirements. They have trained their minds to give them the will power to succeed. They have found the best methods to do this, so they visualize and expect it will happen. Thousands of people who are not necessarily athletes wish to lose weight and keep it off, but often they are incapable of doing so. They cannot visualize the weight loss. You will often hear people say "I would like to lose twenty pounds, but I just can't. They cannot visualize it happening and it doesn't. Anyone is capable of losing weight, but you must visualize it happening and then take the right steps to be successful. Whether you are dropping weight for the Olympic trials or you just want to look and feel better, you are more likely to do it if you visualize it happening.

Long term visualization also works. See yourself in five years. Where do you want to be? If you want to make the cut on an NFL team, and you need to weigh 30 pounds more, run a 40 half a second faster, and bench press 225 pounds 40 times, then start seeing it now. If you have no goals and can't see them happening, they won't happen. Practice visualization constantly. See yourself getting a base hit, sinking a putt, making a free throw. Your body will follow what you visualize in practice.

Whatever you prepare to do you should practice in your mind.

You are about to run a mile and want to do it in six minutes. Map it out in your mind. The first quarter mile must be run in 1-1/4 minutes. The second- and third quarter miles must clock at 1-1/2 minutes each. Finally, you must finish with a 1-3/4 minutes fourth quarter mile. You just ran a six minute mile. You ran it in your mind before you even started. You knew you would succeed because your mind had already seen it. It is imperative that athletes always see themselves winning and achieving. Talk to yourself and eliminate negative words such as can't and cannot from your vocabulary. When you go to bat, say something positive. "I know I can, I know I can I know I can." Say it silently, over and over again, as it happens.

·CHAPTER FIVE·

DESIRE

To be successful you need to have a burning desire to be a champion. You must have a desire for success that is comparable to the desire you would have for air if you were drowning. The desire to win is generated in your mind and your mind must be trained daily. Negative thoughts and words must be eliminated and your mind must be totally engrossed in the thoughts of the rewards for victory.

There is no amount of money or wealth that will compare to the fulfillment of being a champion. There is no political office, no position of power, no position of a king or leader that can compare to being a champion. Ted Arcidi wanted to be the first man to bench press 700 pounds and he put his life on hold to pursue that goal. Why? Because he wanted to be someone, he wanted to reach the stars; he wanted to leave his mark on the earth.

God wants us to be winners and to be great. He gave us life. What we do with our lives is what we give back to him. He also gave us our most valuable resources. He blessed us with astonishing brains to contemplate, plan, and execute where we want to go. It is a personal compass that can lead us to victory. We can be imprisoned, tortured, lose our freedom and even our physical limbs, but something that no dictator, no evil person, no enemy can take from us are our thoughts. As long as you can breathe your mind can think and you are in command of what you do. No one else can think for you. NO ONE!!

Cody Colchado was blind and still competed in world powerlifting meets. Even though he couldn't see, he could still think and he didn't break instead he broke records. You can do that also, you just have to want it badly enough. Never give up on your dreams. Desire will make them come true. Your mind will never fail you. Only you can fail your mind.

The greatest athletes, entrepreneurs, and winners in every endeavor all have the same thing in common. Ted Williams said all he wanted out of life was for people to watch him walk down the street and say "There goes the greatest hitter who ever lived." He said he lived for his next turn at bat. Reggie Jackson said, he would rather it than have sex. Champions get a high from their sport that no drug can ever replace. But, you have to want to win. You have to be willing to sacrifice and put in the work. The athlete with more desire will beat the athlete who is more genetically gifted every time. When you are in a fight, a game, or contest and you have to go deep down within yourself you need the heart of a Lion and a desire to get you over the top. When you are fatigued and need superhuman effort to win, when giving up would be so much easier, your desire will save the day and make you a winner. Many apparently inferior athletes have beaten better ones apparently because of tremendous desire. You must train your mind to want the prize.

·CHAPTER SIX·

TRAIN HARD

I f you want to be a champion you have to train hard, train properly and love what you are doing. There is no way you can reach your potential greatness without desire. Desire separates champions from contenders. Desire is what makes good players great. Desire is a factor that no top athlete can do without. Desire to play, to excel, to become better makes your sport more enjoyable and the more enjoyable it is, the better you will be.

Larry Bird played 12 seasons in the NBA, all for the Boston Celtics. He was an All-Star every year and won three most-valuable player awards and three NBA championships. Larry Bird was not the most-gifted athlete to ever play the game, in fact, some people said he had no natural talent at all. He was not particularly fast and couldn't jump very high yet he became one of the greatest players to ever play the game. He simply outworked his competitors, and it paid off. Larry Bird said when he was a boy he would always shoot another shot, stay a little longer, work a little harder, because he knew if he stopped practicing there was another kid somewhere who would put the extra work in. Remember, if you are not giving it everything you have in practice, someone else is. If you want to go party instead of hit the road and run, someone else will outwork you. Don't shirk training, it leads to quitting and that is a hard habit to break.

There is a myth about the natural player. Top athletes may in some cases appear to have more God given ability than others, but that is not what makes the difference. The difference is work ethic and mind set. The best athletes, with few exceptions, are the ones that work the hardest. Jerry Rice is one of the greatest if not the greatest wide receiver to play in the NFL. He played 20 seasons, was All-Pro 12 times, and won three super bowl rings. He is the all-time NFL leader in receptions, receiving yards and touchdowns. Did you know Jerry Rice did not play division 1 college football and when he was drafted he reportedly ran only a 4.71 40? A Hall of F ame career did not appear to be in his future. Jerry Rice was not the most gifted or fastest wide receiver in the NFL, but he outworked his competitors. Joe Montana, the Quarterback, who threw to him for many of his All-Pro seasons, said he was the hardest worker he had ever seen. Before he married he told his fiancée that they would not be taking vacations after the season like most other players because he would be spending his time training. His commitment, his work ethic, and his desire to be the best, enabled him to play for twenty seasons.

Players that last and have long careers always stay in top shape. Players like Karl Malone, John Stockton, Kareem Abdul Jabbar, Merlin Olsen, and Nolan Ryan stayed on top for years because of their work ethic. Karl Malone scored over 36,000 points in his career; Kareem Abdul Jabbar scored more than 38,000! John Stockton had over 15,000 assists and 3000 steals. Merlin Olsen played in fourteen Pro Bowls and Nolan Ryan struck out 5714 batters!

How can this be done if you do not work hard? Most players would be overjoyed to have half the accomplishments these Hall of Famers have. If you do not put in the work someone with less talent will beat you, be more successful than you, and last longer than you. There is no way to get around this. There are thousands of people no one has ever heard of who could have been champions, but were not willing to put in the work. These people had great genetics and incredible ability, but did not make it because of their lack of motivation to train or you could say the weakness of their minds. Desire and work ethic come from within, and you have to train your mind to love the work and want to be on the practice field. The journey will be much more enjoyable with desire and work ethic.

Control your mind or your mind will control you, and it's not likely to do what you want. Love your sport, love the work, and look at all the benefits you will receive from achieving. You can have everything you want in life by understanding and properly training and utilizing your mind. A great marriage, family, children and your sports dreams can come true. People will tell you these things cannot co-exist, but they most certainly can.

·CHAPTER SEVEN·

DO NOT QUIT

There is no way you will become a champion if you quit. You probably won't even get a chance to be a champion if you have that mentality. Not quitting is a decision of the mind and it means more than just deciding you will attend practice every day. That is a good first step, but it is only that, the first step. You have to decide you will give it everything you have every day you are there. The mind quits first, not the body. The mind tells the body whether to continue or to stop. A decision to finish a marathon or to fight through the final round is made in the mind. Don't quit. Your mind must be trained to keep going and your body will follow.

Quitting is a hard habit to break. The more you do it, the easier it becomes. Jersey Joe Walcott fought for the world boxing heavyweight championship four times, and lost. Finally, he won, on his fifth attempt. His desire to hold the World Champion belt was so powerful he didn't care how many times he had to fight to get it. Every champion has had to go through some level of failure to become the best. The greatest athletes and teams ever assembled have almost always been beaten.

When you watch Major League Baseball's World Series or the NBA's championships remember, these teams have lost many games before getting to the championship series. It must be accomplished in the proper order: persistence, effort, then success. Champions don't care how many times they have to try to win the prize. They don't care how long it takes. They refuse to quit. In fact quitting doesn't even enter their minds.

Baseball pitcher Jim Morris was drafted by the Milwaukee Brewers in the 1983 amateur draft. He was the 4th pick in the first round of the January secondary draft. He suffered many injuries while in the Minor Leagues and was traded to the Chicago White Sox in 1988. He was given a free agent release in 1989 and was out of baseball. After ten years, he decided he still wanted to chase his dream so he made a comeback with the Tampa Bay Devil Rays in 1999. This seemed like a ridiculous idea to many who believed his decision to quit was the right decision and he shouldn't be trying again. But, he would not quit and he finally played his first major league game in 1999 at age 35. His comeback, that many thought to be a joke, had become a reality. He played for two years and was paid more than $200,000 at an age considered old in most professional team sports. He proved to himself and the world that he wasn't a quitter as he chased and realized his dream.

George Foreman retired from professional boxing in 1977. He had already made his mark having won the World Heavyweight Championship and having fought many of boxing's legends. He decided to make a comeback in 1987. Most in the boxing world considered this a joke and warned him against it at his age. Why would he do this? He had already accomplished incredible things in boxing. He was ten years older and heavy and out of shape, hardly anyone gave him a chance to regain the heavyweight title, against younger fighters, had anyone but himself. George Foreman knew he could do it and d to quit trying. Seven years later, at age 45, Foreman knocked out Michael Moorer for the World Heavyweight title. Is this unbelievable? No it is believable. It happened because he did not stop trying.

Train your mind. When running, do not let your mind tell you to quit. When lifting weights do not let your mind allow the weight to stall. The mind must tell the body to continue because the mind controls the body like a puppet-master controls a puppet. If you are wrestling, keep on keeping on until the match is over.

Cael Sanderson, a Wasatch County, Utah wrestler did not lose a single wrestling match for his entire college career at Iowa State.

Four years undefeated (1999 – 2002) and four national championships. He went 159 – 0 for the four years and then went on to win a gold medal in the 2004 Olympics in Athens, Greece. He is arguably not only the greatest wrestler ever, but possibly the greatest athlete. Quitting never entered his mind. There is no way he could have won every single one of his collegiate matches and Olympic Gold if he were not willing to give it everything he had. If he had just let down one time, decided to quit doing the things that made him a champion for just one match, he would not have been unbeaten.

Whatever your athletic endeavors don't quit until you reach your goal whether it is to finish that day's practice or win Olympic Gold. There are thousands of people no one has ever heard of because they quit. They didn't achieve their dreams; they didn't win the prize because they just didn't want it bad enough. Keep looking for your opportunity. Sometimes it's just a matter of showing up. You may make the team or position because it was not filled. Champions look for and take opportunities. Many positions on high school teams are vacant because no one signs up. Don't let small opportunities pass you by they will lead to bigger things. Don't quit. Winners never do.

·CHAPTER EIGHT·

HAVE FUN

If you want to excel at what you do you have to love what you do. You must have a passion for it. The more you love and enjoy what you are doing, the better you will perform. That is a good exchange. Many people believe world class athletes must hate to have to work so hard and devote time to their craft; that is rarely true. Many athletes make comebacks late in life not because they need the money but because they just miss playing the game.

Michael Jordan came back to the NBA for the second time at 38 years of age and played for the Washington Wizards. He was obviously not desperate for money as he donated his salary to victims of the September 11 attacks. He had nothing to prove. He had already won six NBA championships and was regarded by many as one of the greatest if not the greatest player who ever lived, but he loved the game so much and saw an opportunity to help others, and just could not stay away.

Ted Williams was arguably the greatest hitter to ever play in the major leagues. He played a full season in 1941 and had a .406 batting average. He's the last player ever to hit over .400 for the season. After leaving the game in 1943 to become a WWII Marine Fighter Pilot, he came back in 1946 and maintained a .300 plus batting average until 1958. He batted .388 in 1957 at 38 years of age. His career batting average was .344, and his on-base-percentage was .482 which is the highest ever. He was the complete hitter, batting for average and power, rarely striking out, and consistently drawing walks because of his discipline at the plate. He reached base almost one out of every two times he batted! Williams loved the game of baseball. He said he lived for his next turn at bat; and, because of his great love for the game, he produced results. You have to live for your next workout, your next fight, your next game, whatever it is you are doing. It should be this way. Life should be an adventure. You should want to train your mind to love what you are doing.

Arnold Schwarzenegger said he had to learn to love leg training to become a complete powerlifter and then bodybuilder. Often times when you go to the gym you hear people complaining. "Oh, not another set"! "Let's get this over with." You should be anxious to get to the gym and hate to leave it. You should love it so much you get a positive euphoric feeling from your activity. What is better than breaking a record, hitting a home run, or standing on a platform and accepting your trophy? All champions have an authentic love for their sport. If you have the opportunity to meet world-class athletes, you will find they can talk about their sport all day long because they are so captivated by it. Some call this an obsession, but passion is more descriptive and, I believe, more accurate. Love your sport. Do not neglect your family or responsibilities but love what you do. The experience is much more enjoyable when you are passionate about what you do.

Vince Lombardi told his players your priorities are God, family and the Green Bay Packers in that order. Players' loved being part of his teams. You will not succeed if you dread going to the ballpark. You will not succeed if you don't like what you are doing and the ride will be a long, unpleasant one. You must choose a sport you love. If you have already chosen it, train your mind to enjoy it every day. Attitude is everything. Your thoughts and words will make a difference.

Make things exciting to improve. Ask your workout partner who's going to squat more today. Have a competition between yourselves and see who can do more. Give yourself something to shoot for. I know from experience that powerlifters love their sport and would compete for nothing. Because that is what most of them do. There is not a lot of money in this sport and what is available is like loose change. Some of the greatest powerlifters who ever lived, men who have broken world records and lifted mind boggling amounts of weight have not made any money doing it.

The people I know, with whom I have worked out, have all given everything they had to this sport because of a powerful inner love for it. There is not tremendous fame or large amounts of money but these monsters do it and love it. If you are involved in a sport that you can make a living at that is great also. Love your sport no matter what you are doing. Nothing can replace what you will get out of it. John Brzenk is considered the greatest arm wrestler who ever lived. He is a legend in his sport probably more dominant than Michael Jordan, Wayne Gretzky and Sugar Ray Robinson combined. But he has only made $15,000 a year doing it. He does it because he loves his sport. He worked at Delta Airlines for over twenty years so he could fly internationally and compete. That is what made him so great. He had fun and fulfilled his dream.

·CHAPTER NINE·

OVERCOMING FEAR

Overcoming fear is totally controlled by the mind. You must learn to control fear. Many fighters have been beaten, not because of lack of preparation or skills but because of fear of

their opponent. Many athletes have not played to their abilities because of fear. Fear of the opposing team or players. Fear of making mistakes. Fear of letting down friends and family. These are legitimate fears that must be overcome.

In an interview with KO magazine a very young Mike Tyson discussed fear. He was incredibly mature about the subject. He said his trainer and father figure Cus D'amato had talked to him about fear. D'Amato told him everyone has the emotion of fear, but not everyone reacts the same. Tyson said there was no difference between a hero and a coward, other than how they responded to situations. He gave an example of two soldiers who are in a battle with bullets flying everywhere. One does what he has to do to survive and beat the enemy. The other breaks down. There is no difference between the two men just what is in their minds that control their actions. Tyson destroyed many opponents throughout his career because they were often times consumed with fear when they fought him. James "Buster" Douglas beat him finally in 1989 even though

Douglas was a 46-1 underdog and not an impressively accomplished fighter. Douglas had no fear. He knew of Tyson's reputation, how formidable he was, and how many fighters feared him. Tyson was an intimidating presence, even to world class fighters, but when Douglas met him for the first time, he said he just saw a shorter man standing next to him. Douglas could not have won the fight if his reaction had been fear. Tyson never showed fear toward an opponent; but, when one showed no fear of him either, things were suddenly much more competitive.

Jeremy Horn is a legendary MMA fighter. One reason for his great success is his willingness to fight anybody. His list of opponents reads like a who's who of MMA. Randy Courtore, Chuck Liddel, Forrest Griffin, Anderson Silva, Dan Severn, Chael Sonnen. He fought and defeated many outstanding fighters and has more than 100 fights in his career. He fought so many times many of his early fights are not recorded. If you were to meet Jeremy you would find him to be as polite a person as you can imagine; but, he fears no one and he instills the same attitude in the fighters he trains. He has fought so long and so often his mind is just set to get in the cage with anyone. He is so respected that Matt Hughes traveled across the country to train with him when preparing for world title fights. Another amazing thing about Jeremy is his longevity. At the writing of this book, Jeremy has been fighting since age 20 in 1996. In those 18 years he has a record of 90 wins, 21 losses, and 5 draws in 116 fights. That doesn't even include the one's that are not recorded.

It is also important to note that when you are not fearful the chances of injury are reduced. This does not mean you use Tombstone Courage and put yourself into dangerous situations, it means you perform properly because you lack fear, and therefore, execute correctly. Executing incorrect fight moves make you much more susceptible to injury. I personally know many of Jeremy Horn's fighters, and the common denominator among them is their willingness to fight anyone. Jake Heun, Damarques Johnson, Nick Rossborough, David Castillo, Amir Killah and many others will never turn down a fight. They have the same concerns and thoughts before fighting as anyone else; but, they get through it because of their mental strength. MMA is a rough sport and may not be for everyone. The same is for football, boxing, wrestling, and other full contact sports; but, if you choose to participate, you will be more likely to succeed if you have no fear. Fear causes you to hesitate when required to exert full physical power. If you are trying to tackle a strong and incredibly quick running back, and you hesitate because of fear of the collision, you will probably miss the tackle and risk injury. This may not come easily to you; but, you must tell yourself mentally you can do it. Ease into your sport and build up your confidence.

The more you participate, the less fear you will have. It is hard to dig in at the batter's box when the opposing pitcher throws near to 100 miles per hour, but if you decide you will take your stance in the batter's box, dig in, and concentrate, you will do better than if you worry about the speed of the ball.

Golf is not considered a dangerous sport, but fear of missing a putt has surely cost many a golfer a championship. You must develop a mentality to do what you need to do in whatever situation you are in whether you are playing golf or fighting in the UFC. Whatever your sport you must prepare mentally. Be smart about it but have no fear.

·CHAPTER TEN·

HOME COURT ADVANTAGE

Home teams win approximately 70% of their games. Why is this? It primarily comes down to player's minds. When a team or person goes to play in someone else's location their bodies do not change: but, their minds do. There may be a few legitimate factors in getting an advantage at home; playing in an area where the altitude is significantly different is one, traveling and officiating bias may be another, but there is seldom anything resulting in an excuse for losing on the road. Surprisingly this seems never to be addressed. I have never read an article or heard anyone speak about overcoming this to any great extent. Perhaps it has happened but I am not aware of it. Athletes lose on the road because of their minds, period. When a professional team goes to play another professional team a few hundred miles away, they are instantly underdogs because they are on the road. What makes this so? When the bell rings or "Play Ball" is roared, there should be only one thing going on in your head, beating your opponent. The crowd should have no e f f e c t o n y o u.

You should be so deep in the zone a bomb could go off and you would not hear it. Train your mind to win on the road. You're the same person even though you are farther from home.

Teams and players lose on the road because of their brain. How many times have you heard a great and respected coach or manager say "If we can split on the road were in good shape." Those words program teams to accept defeat and lose to the same team they would expect to beat at home. Major league baseball teams play 162 games a year. They play 81 games at home and 81 on the road. An absolute mental refusal to lose on the road, even though they do not have the safety net they enjoy at home, could produce what?, Five, ten, even 20 more wins on the road could make the difference between contesting playoff games and sitting home watching them. Unfortunately, it is accepted in sports that you will not play well-enough to win on the road, and no one thinks a thing about it. Be different. Your thoughts will make or break you.

Jackie Robinson was the first player to cross the color line and play in the major leagues in the modern era. He first played in the National League for the Brooklyn Dodgers, beginning in 1947. Larry Doby was the first player in the American League. He played for the Cleveland Indians and signed just eleven weeks after Robinson. Larry Doby is mostly forgotten as he was the second player in the major leagues to cross the color line, but he went through pretty much everything Jackie Robinson did. Both players had the physical skills to excel in baseball, but it was their mental toughness that allowed them to succeed. Everywhere they went they were met with racial slurs and bigotry. They were often banned from entering the hotels in which the other player's stayed. They received death threats and were constantly under severe and biased scrutiny to prove they could play at that level. The prejudice and pressure were enormous. Yet they both not only succeeded but are also now enshrined in the baseball Hall of Fame.

Their experiences and reactions show that athletes can succeed without having ideal circumstances. Indeed they can be successful even in horrible circumstances. Their situation was much harder mentally than just playing road games. Playing on the road you don't get too many fans cheering for you, but you probably won't have people making death threats against you like some people have had.

Many people have survived this type of treatment because of mental toughness. You can train your mind to believe you are the same player away or at home. This is without doubt all within the mind. If you are a coach or mentor to a young player make every effort to instill within your athlete(s) as early as possible that there is no reason they cannot perform on the road or in other pressure situations. Years of being told about the home court advantage programs the body to perform at a lower level when traveling. Your mind can be trained to expect to win on the road, and since your physical skills don't change from home to away, you should never entertain thoughts that you will not perform as well when you are away from home. I believe this is one of the greatest if not the greatest, mental obstacle in all sports; and something that is accepted without a second thought. If you currently think this way, as many athletes do, change your thinking. Train your mind to think victory, no matter where you are playing. Your mind has the capacity to overcome the let-down when the team goes on the road.

·CHAPTER ELEVEN·

DON'T BE A REALIST

Don't be a realist? Why not? What's wrong with being realistic? Well, if you want to truly achieve greatness you must think outside the box. I'm not saying you should begin by taking on the world heavyweight champion; I am saying you have to believe, really believe you can do anything. That can include beating the heavyweight champion of the world, but you have to be smart about it.

I hate hearing people say athletes are born. If you think athletic genetics is absolutely necessary to win, you will never realize your full potential. It's been shown that people can go well beyond their genetic indicators. Anthony Robles won the NCAA division wrestling championships. That means he was the best wrestler in his weight in the entire country, the United States of America, if not the world. Not many people will argue with me that he was not born with superior genetics. In fact, he was born with fewer athletic genes than probably any other wrestler in the entire world. That's because Anthony Robles was born with one leg. Yes you read that correctly. ONE LEG. So I would guess when Anthony Robles decided he could become NCCA Division1 champ he was not much of a realist. I guess when he achieved it he threw the reality of the necessity of great genetics into the garbage.

You are capable of doing anything. Do not let negative thoughts enter your mind disguised as realism. It doesn't matter your background, your experience, your height, your weight or whatever. You can become a champion. You can become great. If we all were realists we would not be living with electricity, TV, the internet or traveling through air and space because all these things were thought to be impossible. Train your mind now to believe that whatever you put your mind to, you can do. Again, don't fight the heavyweight champion your first fight but believe you can get there and win one day, and if you have to fight him, so what? Believe you can beat him because the impossible is achieved every day through the power of the mind.

Jim Abbott became a professional, major league baseball player, and a pretty good one. He played ten years in the major leagues won the rookie of the year award in 1989 and finished third in the voting for the Cy Young award in 1991, when he won 18 games and had a 2.89 E.R.A. He did this having been born without one arm. No genetic advantage there. You cannot be locked into a reality and expect to reach your potential.

Imagine yourself bigger, stronger and quicker than you have ever been before. Do the work. Never shirk the work. If you go against an opponent you feel is more physically gifted than you then find a way to win. You must work harder, you must be smarter, and you must have more heart. All these things come from your mind!

You will hear people tell you all your life that you are not smart enough, big enough, fast enough, strong enough, or whatever to achieve greatness. Do not listen to them. Find a way. One of my good friends and lifting partner, Spencer Westwood, trained alone in his bedroom. After a while, with the majority of his equipment he made himself, he advanced to his shed. He told me he would become a champion. And he did! He made no excuses. He found a way even though his training conditions were laughable! Spencer squatted over 600 and 700 pounds in sanctioned meets while weighing between 148 and 165 pounds!

In the 1980 Olympics, the U.S.A. Hockey Team went against the seemingly invincible U S S R, Russians. The U.S. team was a group of amateurs, mostly college kids, going against the greatest team in the world. The idea that the U.S. team could beat the USSR's professional hockey players, was totally laughable, why not? The Russian team had won the gold medal in the 1956 and the 1964 Olympics and every four years since, until 1980. In the last four Olympics, the Soviet teams had gone 27-1 and had outscored their opponents 175-44.

The Soviets practiced in world class training facilities and played against top opposition. They had many legendary players on the team including Boris Mikhailov, Vladislav Tratiek, Valeri Kharlmalov, and Viacheslov Fetisov. The U.S. team, on the other hand, had one player returning from the 1976 team. In spite of the odds, the U. S. players played the game of their lives and won 4 – 3. Sportscaster Al Michaels, who announced the game, will always be remembered for saying, "Do you believe in miracles!" as time elapsed.

Wilma Rudolf was a poor and sickly child, born in 1940 in Clarksville, Tennessee. She was premature and weighed less than five pounds, at four years of age, she was diagnosed with polio and doctors told her she would never walk. Wilma and her parents persevered. For the next two years, Mrs. Rudolf took her daughter treatment twice a week. They drove fifty miles each way to the hospital that treated her. She was finally fitted with a metal leg brace that enabled her to walk.

She was then taught by doctors and therapists to do physical therapy that she could do with the help of her family. At the age of 12, she began to walk normally again. She began to participate in sports and soon believed she could accomplish anything for which she was willing to fight. In 1960, at the age of 20, and 16 years after being diagnosed with Polio, she became the first American woman to win three gold medals in the Olympics. She won them all in track and field and was told she had become the fastest woman in the world.

Rulon Gardner is another outstanding example of winning against the odds. Like the 1980 U. S. hockey team, he wrestled a Russian opponent, Alexander Karelin, for the Olympic Heavyweight gold metal. Karelin had not lost a match in 13 years and had not given up a point in six. The unrealistic farm boy defeated the Russian and brought the gold medal back to the U. S. and to his home in Wyoming. Never believe you don't have a chance. You always can develop the skills and heart to be a winner!

·CHAPTER TWELVE·

LIVE A MORAL LIFE

What does living a moral life have to do with mental performance? A lot. In fact, it could make the entire difference between becoming a champion and failing to achieve your goals. A recent example of this is Pro Golfer Tiger Woods. Tiger was once golf's "Golden Boy." Almost every week, his game was head and shoulders above everyone else. He was consistently named as the number one golfer in the world, year after year. Then his extra-marital affairs were exposed. His performance on the golf course plummeted. Why? Mentally he had changed. He was not the same golfer. Physically he was the super-pro he had always been, but his mental edge was lost. He had forfeited his concentration. The question naturally arose, what if he had not engaged in this immoral behavior? Did that make a difference? You better believe it! The game he loved was not as much fun anymore.

If you want to be a champion, you must have a clear head. Marital problems, trouble with the law, any kind of behavior that transgresses your personal moral code can cause your mental edge to abandon you. You can't always control other peoples' behavior, but you can control your own. You can live an honest, moral life. The higher you climb on the ladder of success, the more people you will find that are controlled by a moral code. There is a belief that all world class athletes party and sleep around. Some do of course, but few of them last. The list of top athletes that ruined their careers (and lives) is very long and keeps going. Steve Howe, Magic Johnson, Len Bias, Art Schlichter, John Daly, Mike Tyson, Lyle Alzado, Dwight Gooden, Darryl Strawberry, Dennis Mclain. Good grief! How many of them would give much of what they have to do it over? And how about the thousands of talented people who never even made a name for themselves because of unacceptable behavior? There is more untapped physical ability in the worlds' prisons and graveyards than anywhere else. These are people who could have fulfilled their dreams, but never made it because of their inability to control their behavior. Don't make the same mistakes. We are all human and can fall, but you can take precautions to ensure it doesn't happen to you.

Don't even consider entering a situation or circumstance that will bring you down. Associate with winners. If you want to be a champion, or be world class, and if you want to be a winner on the court and off, you must retain that slight edge over your opponents. The more athletes I meet, the more I am surprised at how many did not drink. Why? The edge. If you do drink, be responsible. It's hard to concentrate on your game if you're worrying about what will happen because of your last DUI arrest, not to mention what the media attack will do to you. They can be unmerciful and very unfair. Life never is fair, unfortunately that's just a fact. Stay away from pornography, drugs, excessive drinking, and promiscuous sex. Just how will this behavior affect you?

A disciplined moral life will carry over to sports performance. You should be asleep early every night. You should get a good night's sleep and wake up early every day. There are few occasions you will need to be up past 10pm. Get in this habit. Associate with people who have good morals. Immoral and amoral people will bring you down. Misery loves company.

Josh Hamilton was the first round pick in the 1999 major league baseball draft. He was a sure star who developed a problem. He became addicted to drugs and alcohol. He floundered for years in the minors, not playing in a single major league game. In fact, from

2004 to 2006 he dropped out of baseball completely and didn't even play in the minor leagues. In 2005, he went through rehab. Then in 2007, clean and sober, he began his comeback and the Cincinnati Reds gave him a chance. He moved to the Texas Rangers in 2008 and played for them through 2009. In 2010, still with the Rangers, he was named the American League MVP. He had not only defeated his addiction but also returned to the form that helped him reach the top of his sport as an All-Star and MVP.

If you have addictions or similar problems, now is the time to change them, before it is too late to chase your dreams. Immoral and illegal behavior will destroy you from the neck up and down. Larry Gelwix coached Highland high school's Rugby team from 1976 to 2010. His teams had a combined record of 404 wins and ten losses; and, they won 19 of the 26 USA Rugby championships that were sponsored during that time. He was very demanding with his players and they had to adhere to a strict honor code. They were prohibited from use of drugs, tobacco, or alcohol. The strict code he enforced with his players helped produce these championships. He knew they could become champions if they led moral lives. You can also experience the thrill of being a champion, when you keep your act clean.

• CHAPTER THIRTEEN

COACHING

I f you are a coach who wants to get the most out of your

team and/or individuals you better take this chapter very

seriously. As a coach, you are looked upon as a leader.

You must take control and your players will most likely follow

your every instruction. You will have to exercise your mind for

every strategy, every motivation, and every move, to make your

athletes the best they can be.

The first requirement is to know your sport inside and out. You

need to know every possible training routine there is to make your

players better. You will have to read and research a lot and

take notes on the information you discover Talk with everyone that

can improve your coaching. You also have to be selective where you

get your information. Not all available information is equal. You have

to go with the best information you can find and use it. Do not

overlook something that may help you if you want to win. You need

every advantage possible, no matter how small.

The second requirement for a coach is the need to convince your

people they are the best, then motivate them to believe they

can do anything. This book is a guide for the coach and not just

the athlete. Coaches can refer to all the chapters in this book for specific helps. The chapter on home field advantage is a must. It is a common belief that teams do not win as often on the road. You must change that. If you are a good coach, your players will listen to you. Your fighters or competitors believe what you say. They see you as an expert because you are a coach. Little league coaches are often times just the parent who has time to help and is willing to do it. This kind of coach is making a sacrifice for others but may not know a whole lot about the sport he is coaching. If this is the case, you may not be capable of teaching all the skills to your players, but you can always teach them to believe in themselves. This is extremely important. If you and your athletes don't believe in yourselves you will never reach your potential, no matter how much you know the game and how much work you put into it. Regardless of a coach's knowledge the players look at him as knowing all and can do no wrong. This is true at most any level. The athlete's mind is controlled to a large extent by the coach, and the mind controls the body.

Vince Lombardi was in my opinion the greatest coach who ever lived. He was a strict disciplinary who demanded respect from his players. He told his players there will be three things in your life from now on: God, your family, and the Green Bay Packers, in that order. Lombardi coached in the 1960's when m any athletes were becoming un-disciplined and an anything goes attitude was prevalent. He refused to change his coaching style to fit in; and, he was a fantastic motivator. He took the Green Bay Packers to the first two Super Bowls and won them both, without inheriting a powerhouse team. His most memorable speech, number one, is widely used today by coaches and others trying to motivate people. Most people are familiar with at least part of it. For your perusal, here it is again.

"Winning is not a sometime thing; it's an all the time thing. You don't win once in a while; you don't do things right once in a while; you do them right all the time. Winning is a habit. Unfortunately, so is losing.

There is no room for second place. There is only one place in my game, and that's first place. I have finished second twice in my time at Green Bay, and I don't ever want to finish second again. There is a second place bowl game, but it is a game for losers played by losers. It is and always has been an American zeal to be first in anything we do, and to win, and to win, and to win.

Every time a football player goes to play his trade he's got to play from the ground up---from the soles of his feet right up to his head. Every inch of him has to play. Some guys play with their heads. That's O.K. You've got to be smart to be number one in any business. But more importantly, you've got to play with you heart, with every fiber of your body. If you're lucky enough to find a guy who plays with a lot of head and a lot of heart, he's never going to come off the field second.

Running a football team is no different than running any other organization - an army, a political party or business. The principles are the same. The object is to win --- to beat the other guy. Maybe that sounds hard or cruel. I don't think it is.

It is a reality of life that men are competitive and the most-competitive games draw the most-competitive men. That's why they are there --- to compete and to know the rules and objectives when they get in the game. The object is to win fairly, squarely, by the rules --- but to win.

And in truth, I've never known a man worth his salt who in the long run, deep down in his heart, didn't appreciate the grind, the discipline. There is something in good men that really yearns for discipline and the harsh reality of head to head combat.

I don't say these things because I believe in the "brute" nature of man or that men must be brutalized to be combative. I believe in God, and I believe in human decency. But I firmly believe that any man's finest hour, the greatest fulfillment of all that he holds dear, is that moment when he has worked his heart out in a good cause and lies exhausted on the field of battle --- victorious."

The greatest coaches ever, Vince Lombardi, John Wooden, Bill Walsh, Angelo Dundee, Cus D'Amato knew they had to get in their players and fighters heads. All the practice in the world will not replace mindset. Learn how to control your mind and pass it on.

·CHAPTER FOURTEEN·

HAVE A PLAN

If you want to succeed you must create a plan. You map it out first in your mind; you then put it on paper and then follow through. In this process, you should think big.

Remember, small thoughts generate small results. You will not achieve more than you believe you can. So plan the ending of your plan to be huge. You will not rise to a victorious level unless you believe you can and then take the steps necessary to get there.

If you bench press 250 pounds and want to bench 300 you need to make a routine, a time period, and dedicate yourself to doing the work. You must also believe totally that you will reach your goal. The key to athletic success is to gather the right information, make a plan, and stick with it. And remember, THINK BIG! If nobody laughs at your goal maybe you're not thinking big enough. No one just stumbles upon or is given success.

You may be given endless amounts of opportunities, but no one can do the training for you. Only you can make it happen. Develop the right plan, do the right physical training and train your mind to not accept defeat. Your mind will be the deciding factor for you to win. It will be a factor for your start. It will be a factor for your progress and it will be a factor determining whether you succeed or quit. Your mind controls everything you do or say. You are in control of your mind and no one can take that control from you without your permission. You may not have complete control of anything else in your life, but no one can think for you. No one knows what is going on inside your head but you.

Make your plan properly, so you can be somebody, so you will improve and achieve. You should have short-term and long-term goals. In order to realize success with your long-term goals, you need to first achieve your short-term goals. If you want to play in the NFL and you're still in high school, you should create a plan to achieve your long term goal. Hopefully, you have the support of friends and family. If not, make different friends. You can't change your family, but you don't have to listen to them if their advice is negative. You will have to find the best possible coaching. You will then need to follow his/her advice for your workouts and for your eating habits. Oh---and you had better immediately give up partying. Start now to follow a workout schedule to make you quicker, faster, and stronger. When you get to college, follow the same advice and you can realize your dream of making an NFL team. You've heard the saying, "If you fail to plan, you plan to fail." It is an athletic truism, as sure as day turns to night.

On June 19, 1936, German boxing strongman, Max Schmeling fought World Champion Joe Louis in Yankee Stadium in New York City. Louis was a heavy 10-1 favorite to win this fight. Schmeling said before the fight, "I see something...." He would tell no one what he had seen, but it was realized later that he had noticed that Louis had a habit of dropping his left hand when throwing a right-hand punch. Schmeling trained perfectly to take advantage of Louis's habit and dropped him in the fourth round. Joe Louis had never been knocked down before. Schmeling controlled the fight from then on and knocked Louis out in round twelve. Schmeling had made a plan that gave him victory over Louis. A rematch was fought on June 22, 1938. Louis knocked out Schmeling in the first round. Louis learned from his mistake and made sure he had a plan to win this time. He trained incredibly hard for this fight and made sure he would not give Schmeling the opportunity to beat him. He also trained correctly to eliminate his habit of dropping his left hand

and leaving himself open. You must have a plan, a strategy to win. Map it out in your mind, write it down and execute it.

When Roger Bannister ran the first four-minute mile on May 6, 1954, it didn't happen by accident. He made a plan and followed it. Bannister planned the race carefully and used two pacemakers named Chris Chataway and Chris Brasher. Brasher took the lead with Bannister behind him and Chataway in third place. When Brasher tired Chataway would take over. They helped push him over the four-minute mark. Bannister had also trained specifically to run under four minutes and his plan was realized on that day.

Boxers and MMA fighters have long drawn out plans to become champions. The best ones first seek out the best training they can, they fight their way in the amateurs and then become professional. They gradually fight better fighters until they reach the top. Every great achievement in life and sports is accomplished with a plan. Success does not just happen because of luck. Whatever your goals are, develop and follow a plan!

·CHAPTER FIFTEEN·

OVERCONFIDENT

Being confident is a good thing. You must be confident and believe completely in yourself. However, overconfidence can be a bad thing. This doesn't mean one should not be confident in difficult situations. A certain level of confidence is necessary for every challenge. Overconfidence, however, can help to bring you down if not properly handled. Even if you lack confidence and doubt yourself when faced with a hard challenge; and your own confidence is lessened by others suggesting you cannot achieve the goal you have set for yourself.

In all these situations, you should and must believe in yourself. The danger in overconfidence is when you do not follow your game plan, you do not train hard enough or you underestimate your opponent. This can put a loss on your record. Many great athletes and teams have been beaten because they have not prepared well enough because they thought they were so good they could not lose. Respect every opponent and train for every competition to be your best. If you don't, you may well lose the event that was considered a sure win for you. Losses in these situations are not uncommon. I've referred to a number of them in this book, such as the Joe Louis vs. Max Schmeling fight in 1938 and the "Miracle on Ice" in the 1980 Olympics.

Showboating and goofing off will also lead to failure. In practice or competition you should never allow yourself to become a comedian. You may have seen others perform as clowns and you thought how fun and colorful they were. They may have gotten away with it, but that doesn't mean you will. Many have not. Anderson Silva was believed by many to be the best pound for pound MMA fighter in the world when he was knocked out by Chris Weidman. He was showboating and not taking the fight seriously and paid the price for it. Rocky Marciano was always in tip top shape. He finished his career 49-0 because he never took an opponent lightly and trained hard for every fight. He was never overconfident and his perfect record reflects it.

Jimmy Braddock fought heavily favored Max Baer in 1935. Braddock was given no chance to beat the champion. It made sense, Braddock had lost 25 fights and Baer was world champion. It was considered such a joke for Braddock to fight for the title that some odds makers had him a 15-1 underdog. Well, Jimmy Braddock won that bout. He beat Max Baer that night in front of a shocked crowd in Madison Square Garden in New York City. It was believed and reported that Baer had not trained seriously for the fight and his overconfidence cost him the title.

Take every opponent you have very seriously. Never start thinking you don't have to train as hard for your next game or fight. Maybe you're about to face a 0-12 o p p o n e n t and think you can stay out late partying or miss a few workouts or eat junk food for a while. This thinking will probably cost you and may get you into habits that will ruin your career. Remember someone out there will do things right if you won't and they will be holding the trophy i n s t e a d o f y o u . Train your mind and get in the habit of being confident, not overconfident. Believe in yourself completely. It doesn't matter what the odds are or how hard the task and it doesn't matter if people tell you that you can't make it. Believe you can and train accordingly then you will. Embrace confidence but deplore overconfidence. Get rid of it or it will take you down.

·CHAPTER SIXTEEN·

TRAIN LIKE YOU COMPETE

When you are in training you need to train as if you are competing. You have to prepare to compete with a specific opponent or competition. General training has its place, but it is not when you are preparing for a competition with a specific opponent. Your subconscious mind will remember how you trained and will use that information to respond appropriately to a given opponent. Take this in and your mind will respond accordingly. Muscle memory will perform in competition as you trained in practice. If you are going to face a pitcher who throws a lot of breaking balls, you need to spend your time hitting good breaking balls, prior to facing this him. If you don't, you will suffer through some frustrating at bats. It might be more fun to practice by hitting fastballs, but by the time the game starts it will be too late to adjust your swing for the breaking stuff.

Vince Lombardi said perfect practice makes perfect. You have to be smart about what you are doing. If you are a boxer or an MMA fighter, spar with people who are similar to your next opponent. If you will be fighting a taller opponent with a good jab find someone who is physically similar and has a long good jab. If your next opponent has good take down skills find someone else who does and practice defending takedowns. When you get to the ring or cage, you will be ready. Your subconscious will remember what you have practiced and your body will follow the direction from your subconscious mind. You may practice hard and give it everything you have, but if you don't train correctly your body will not respond correctly. Study your sport and your opponents and train properly. Repetitive training will train your mind to continually control your body.

Muhammad Ali sparred with Larry Holmes, Michael Weaver and Michael Dokes. All held world championship belts at one time. Ali knew it was not an easy day's work getting in the ring with these guys, but he knew he had to have the best sparring partners, whose fighting styles would help him beat his opponents.

When Hank Aaron first came to professional baseball he could not hit a change-up, so he spent the off-season working on that deficiency and it paid off. Work on your weaknesses as well as your strengths. It's easy to work on what you excel at, but if you neglect other parts of you game they will be exploited. If you can't hit a knuckleball and you don't practice to correct that, you will see a lot of knuckleballs thrown at you. Remember that every time you practice, and you will train your mind to react properly and to provide the proper signals to your body.

·CHAPTER SEVENTEEN·

TOMBSTONE COURAGE

T here is a saying in law enforcement known as "Tombstone Courage." It refers to a decision by an officer to attempt an act of bravery in order to resolve a risky situation. It's called Tombstone Courage because it can get you killed. It's an unwise action because it's not only risky but also may not resolve the situation. Unfortunately, police officers have died because they took an overly courageous approach to a situation that could have been handled differently.

Courage is an absolute necessity in life and in sports, but you have to be smart about it. Cowardice will get you killed and make you lose and Tombstone Courage can do the same. In athletics, Tombstone Courage can cost you a win, a championship, and maybe your career. Billy Conn fought Joe Louis on June 18, 1941. Conn, a light-heavyweight fighter, went against Louis, the Heavyweight Champion of the World, to try to take the heavyweight belt from him. Conn actually weighed less than the 175 light-heavyweight limit and Louis was around 200 pounds. Louis, who was one of the greatest fighters of all time and had tremendous punching power was highly favored to beat the smaller Conn; but Conn boxed Louis from the beginning and after 12 round he had a clear lead. With only three rounds to go the 50,000 plus fans at the Polo Grounds in New York City thought they were going to see one of the greatest upsets in sports history. And they probably would have, but Conn decided to use Tombstone Courage, or as he later said, "The Irish in me." Conn abandoned his superior boxing skills and quickness which had given him control of the fight and tried to knock Louis out. Instead, Louis knocked Conn out in the 13th round. Conn was an exceptional fighter; one of the best to ever lace on a pair of gloves. But, on this night, his great courage got the best of him.

Fear should have no place in your life but be smart how you do things. There is more than one way to win. Muhammad Ali hardly threw a punch against George Foreman until the 8th round of their fight, but he had a game plan to beat the ferocious Foreman. Foreman was so exhausted by round 8; Ali was able to KO him. Foreman had not counted on having to do anything but hit his opponent and watch him fall. After all, he had just knocked out the legendary and at the time seemingly invincible, Joe Frazier, who had already defeated Ali and was a large favorite to beat Foreman. Foreman knocked him down six times and afterwards felt no human being could withstand his punches. A reminder, overconfidence can kill.

Many athletes who have showboated came up short because of their overconfidence. Stick to your game plan. If you are winning stay the course. Mentally practice this skill and you won't lose when you should win; because you want to show off or think your opponent is already beaten. Stay in control. Do not fear your opponent but respect his abilities. Know you can beat him but you have to have the correct training and game plan. You should NEVER, NEVER take an opponent lightly, no matter his/her reputation.

You need to have great confidence, but you must also train as if your life depends on winning. Countless champions have been defeated because they trained half-heartedly. You need to give every game, every fight, and every practice all you can give. Upsets happen in sports because one of the competitors wanted it more. Desire can overcome talent and desire can be destroyed by allowing yourself to be overconfident. When it's game time and you are not mentally and physically prepared, it's too late. Don't look back and wonder, what if? Train your mind every day to give everything you have to every practice, match, and game. Don't underestimate your opponent and assume he will not underestimate you. That mental preparation could be the difference. It's especially important to not use Tombstone Courage when injured. The mind will allow you to overcome horrific injuries, but you have to be smart about things. If you are injured, no matter the seriousness, believe you will come back, believe you will overcome it, but do not use Tombstone Courage to get there. If you are injured get the best help available and someone who believes as strongly as you that you will come back as good or even better, than before, but give yourself time to recover.

Many high school athletes try to come back too soon and re-injure themselves. If injured as a teenager, you have many years left. Mike Saunders, one of the lifters I train with, suffered a severe injury from squatting. He was not prepared to use the equipment and amount of weight for the lift. Mike fears no weight but in this case he should have bypassed the lift. Mike would not give up though. He took the time to recover and get healthy and believed he would. Now he is a world class squatter and holds National records in powerlifting. Many other athletes have done the same. Use common sense.

A young Willie Mays almost made a mistake when he was suffering from a sore arm. He had heard that the great Yankee centerfielder, Joe DiMaggio, had a similar injury during a world series and was afraid base runners might take advantage of him because they knew of his injury. He decided after pre- game warmups he would throw from center field to home to let them know he still could throw. In a regular season game, Mays discussed doing the same thing but was told not to by his manager. His situation was not the same; he still had a long season ahead. DiMaggio, on the other hand, had the entire off-season to rest his arm and recuperate. Mays chose to not risk it. His arm healed and he too became one of the great players of all time. Tombstone Courage could have hurt him.

Believe you can overcome injuries because you can. Horrific injuries are overcome through the power of our minds and belief our bodies can heal. But be smart about it. Get the best help available and listen to it.

Dennis Byrd was partially paralyzed after suffering a broken neck while playing for the New York Jets in 1992. Doctors told him he would never walk again. On September 5, 1993 Dennis

Byrd walked onto the field on his own power for the Jets home opener as their honorary captain. He credited his recovery to a belief he would recover and a faith in God. Dennis Byrd refused to accept life living in a wheelchair.

You can overcome most things in this life with mental strength. Use valor and the right kind of courage to do so.

·CHAPTER EIGHTEEN·

PRESSURE AND STRESS

Many athletes never reach their potential or perform in situations because they have too much mental stress and pressure. You have to train your mind to perform no matter what and you need to learn to prioritize and put things into perspective. If you place a 10 foot long 2 x 4 on the ground, you should be able to easily walk the length of it without falling. But, if you secure that same 2 x 4 between two buildings and try to walk the length of it, it will be much more difficult. The mind changes because of circumstances.

Some athletes perform well in pressure situations, some do not. Basketball free throws, football field goals, golf putts, soccer and hockey penalty shots, etc. are all pressure situations and they are usually made or missed because of your mental state. The athlete has practiced and prepared physically but if the mind is not prepared the body will often fail. You have to repeatedly practice visualizing success. Whatever you participate in, you must mentally rehearse for success. Constantly affirm to yourself, "I will succeed. I will succeed. I will succeed."

The best way to handle stress in general and reduce pressure in a given situation is to put things in the right perspective. Remember, you are playing a game or s p o r t s activity. This is not life or death and if you put unnecessary pressure on yourself to succeed, you will create stress and will probably not enjoy the game. This mental condition may also cost you a victory. In the chapter "Have Fun," it states you will perform better if you love what you're doing. Have fun playing and competing. Give it everything you have but don't let your opponent get up on you because you are consumed with worry about winning and performing. Win or lose your dog will not die, hunger and famine will not go away, cancer will not be cured and world peace will not suddenly be ours. Do not stress, just decide you will perform at your best and make the play and that is that.

Tony Horton is a mostly forgotten baseball player who played for the Boston Red Sox and Cleveland Indians from 1964 to 1970. He was a solid player, with a great future, but he unexpectedly left the game during the 1970 season when he was just 25 years old. Tony had become an emotional wreck from continually stressing about how he would perform. He reached the point where he could no longer handle going to the ballpark every day. He never talked about why he quit, choosing to just leave baseball behind. Apparently the game was no longer fun for him because he couldn't handle the stress. If you're not enjoying what you are doing you are doing something wrong and will never perform up to your own expectations. Do not do this to yourself or, if you are a coach or parent, to your players or children. Life should be an adventure and every moment should be worth living. Have fun, do things right, work hard and you will be a champion. Many players will become much better if they can overcome the uncontrollable pressure and stress. Many rookies have a tremendous desire and feel t h e weight on their shoulders to become great at their sport, but they perform poorly because of the pressure they feel. Their second and third years sometimes are much better if they can rid themselves of the intense pressure they feel as rookies; but, this doesn't always work.

Carl Yastrzemski began his rookie season with the Boston Red Sox in 1961 and he took the position previously held by the baseball icon, Ted Williams, in the outfield. Williams was considered by most to be the greatest player the Red Sox ever had. He had already become a baseball legend in Boston and the rest of the country. The pressure on Yastrzemski was immense, both by the fans and the media. His first year wasn't something to write home about. He batted only .266 with 11 home runs; but "Yaz" did not fold. The following season the pressure of Williams' legend was not as intimidating and he had learned to handle the many comparisons thrown at him. His average improved to just below .300 and he contributed 19 home runs and 94 RBI's. He went on to a 23-year career with the Boston Red Sox and in 1989 was voted into the Hall of Fame to be honored alongside Williams. He finished his baseball career having been an 18 time All-Star with nine Golden Gloves and with membership in the elite 3000 hit club. He is currently ranked at number 8 on that list. He did not let pressure and stress stop him.

Mickey Mantle replaced Joe DiMaggio in the outfield for the New York Yankees in 1952 when DiMaggio retired. What a pressure situation that was, replacing a baseball icon on the New York Yankees! Mantle had a poor rookie year, but like "Yaz" who followed him by 9 years, was able to overcome the challenge of following a legend and became a Hall of Famer also. He also hit more home runs in the World Series than any other player. When the pressure was on, he excelled.

In 1991, BYU Quarterback Steve Young followed Joe Montana as the quarterback for the San Francisco 49ers. Montana became a legend while he was still playing, having won four Super Bowls with the 49ers. Talk about pressure to perform! Young had a rough start and almost lost his starting position to Steve Bono, but Young withstood the pressure and secured his position and in 1994 returned the 49ers to a Super Bowl victory. Each of the afore' mentioned athletes overcame significant struggles with pressure to perform and became great athletes in their own right.

It was partly from learning how to better play the game but mostly they were able to cope with the great mental pressure to perform. If you are ever in a similar situation believe from the get-go you can get the job done. As soon as you do, you will succeed. Stay with it when the pressure is on, get rid of stress and be mentally strong!

·CHAPTER NINETEEN·

DISTRACTIONS

One of the worst things that can happen to an athlete is to perform poorly because of a distraction. Distractions affect the mind and will often change your performance level because concentration has been lost or fear has enveloped you. When competing in an athletic event, you must be totally focused on what you are doing and you must eliminate everything from your mind that keeps you from such concentration. You should be thinking about your performance and nothing else. Other thoughts or worries, big or small, need to be left out of the gym or off the playing field until you are finished. Many athletes perform at a lower level because of distractions. Athletes encounter many distractions, some are serious and others are trivial. Unfortunately, both kinds of distraction can have a negative impact on your performance.

You can and should devote all your energy to solving any off court problems, but the playing field is not the place for it. If you have had a disagreement with your significant other, have a financial problem or are going through some rough family matters, etc. Whatever the problem do what you have to do to fix it. If someone is booing you or there is something going on out of the ordinary on the field concentrate on your game.

On June 12, 1989 Thomas Hearns was going to fight Sugar Ray Leonard in a rematch for which Hearns had waited eight years. It was to be one of the biggest fights of his career. He had lost previously to Leonard, who was a boxing legend, and he was consumed with the desire to avenge it. Leonard was an enormous favorite and was expected to win easily. Two days before the fight, Thomas Hearn's brother was arrested for suspicion of murder. This was a terrible tragedy and it would have been completely understandable if Hearns had pulled out of the fight. The expected thing for Hearns to do was to postpone the fight. However, Hearns knew pulling out of the fight could not help or change the situation so he decided to continue. Hearns knocked Leonard down twice and the judges ruled the fight a draw. Most observers thought Hearns had won and Leonard later admitted he felt Hearns had beaten him this time. The point is, however that Hearns had incredible mental strength to be able to perform in spite of family tragedy. No one would have blamed him if he pulled out, but he decided to continue and fought an excellent fight. Now with the fight over he could concentrate totally on the family situation.

There is a time and place for everything. Make sure you have your priorities in order, but there will be times you must play with distractions. Sometimes they may be horrific. Hopefully, they will not be tragic. But, regardless the severity of the distraction, you must clear your head to compete. If you can't, you help no one especially yourself. You will often play among hostile fans. Again this should not affect you play. You will play in bad weather, extreme heat and extreme cold. Train your mind to get through this.

Jack Johnson was the world heavyweight champion at the turn of the 20th century. He held the heavyweight championship belt from 1908 to 1915. He was the first non-white champion at a time when few professional sports were integrated. Boxing was, but racial tensions were so severe that race riots had taken place after Johnson won. Johnson received constant death threats and had to live knowing his life was in danger every time he fought. When he did fight, he was bombarded with profanity and every name in the book, from the first bell to the last. In order to concentrate on the task at hand, he had to block out everything and focus on what his opponent was doing. Despite all this, he was still able to excel.

You will go through a lot of distractions when you participate in sports, but you will probably not have to worry about losing your life because you participated in a contest. Minimize your distractions, whether big or small, and they will hopefully not be so severe that they impact your preparation and skills.

Great athletes such as Ted Williams serve in the military and have had experiences most of us will never imagine. The mental strength military combatants must have is much tougher than anything you will deal with as an athlete. Williams actually served in both World War II and what was called the Korean Conflict, and has been called the real "John Wayne." He was a Navy aviator in the U.S. Marine Corps and flew 39 combat missions over Korea. His baseball accomplishments are legendary and surely serving that time made him mentally strong as a baseball player. There can be a lot of distractions in sports, but they don't compare to putting your life on the line in fighting a war. He won the American League batting title at forty years of age after serving all his time in the U. S. Military. He was the last player to bat .400 for an entire season and that is a mark many think will never be equaled again. I believe it will but someone has to have the mental resolve to believe they can reach it.

·CHAPTER TWENTY·

ASSOCIATE WITH WINNERS

If you want to be a winner and think like a winner you have to associate with winners. Winners have a way about them that everyone should strive to emulate. They are always looking for ways to win rather than finding excuses why they can't. This will have a positive effect on you, your mindset and your performance.

I remember the first time I competed in the World Bench Press and Deadlift Championships in Reno, Nevada in 2002. The atmosphere was incredible. I was rubbing shoulders with champions from all over the globe. There were lifters from in Europe, South and Central America, Asia, Canada, India and all over the world. Many champions, of all ages and weight classifications, came from the various states in the U.S. What a feeling it was to be part of it. Each one had to believe in himself to even get there. This atmosphere rubs off on you. Unfortunately, negativity will also impact you. Stay away from the excuse makers. Their attitude is a disease that affects not only them but also those around them. There is no time to lose. God put us here to win, not to squander away this great gift of life. Associating with small-minded and weak-thinking people will have a negative impact on you. If you have friends or even family members that are negative, try to dissuade them from their negativity and persuade them to think positively. If you can't, get as many miles away from them as possible. They will bring you down and you may not be able to recover. They may have good intentions, but they are misguided. You must follow your dreams, not someone else's, and family and peer support are critical. This is the reason the best players have the best coaches, the best mentors, and supportive family members.

Don't settle for mediocrity. You are better than that. Think big and don't let others stop you. People will tell you to play it safe and to chase an average job, an average goal, and an average dream. If that's what you do, that's what you will get. You will then spend the rest of your life wondering, what if? Give your dream a chance. Even if you don't make it you will always know you left nothing in the tank. Remember, if nobody laughs at your dream it probably isn't big enough. Choose friends and seek-out people who have high goals and want great things in life; and those who also want to see you achieve. Seek out the best coaches, workout partners, and mentors. Winning is contagious; but, unfortunately, so is losing.

Get in the habit of associating with winners and winners will gravitate to you. You will become the person other winners will seek out and look up to. There is no time to lose. As stated previously, sometimes you will be in a position that you cannot avoid negative influences. Throughout your life, you will have to be around negative people at times. Co-workers, family members or classmates may tell you that you won't make it. Like the previous paragraph says, if you can't avoid them remember don't listen to them. No matter who you are, you will come across people who will tell you that you won't make it. You're too slow, too short, too small, too old, whatever negativity they can throw at you. If you buy into that attitude, why even try?

Athletes like Spud Webb the 5' 7 NBA player who won the NBA slam dunk competition, and Tom Dempsey, who was born with no toes on his kicking foot but made the longest field goal in NFL history at sixty-three yards. Both of these athletes were told throughout their lives, they would never make it. The negative criticism didn't stop them.

If 999 of 1000 people tell you that you can't, listen to the one person who says that you can and make him your friend. The higher level of success you attain, in athletics and in life, the more powerful the belief that superior achievement is possible. Not only for one's self, but also for others. This is not a coincidence. The mind dictates how far the body will go and what it will achieve. Seek out positive people. Winners and successful people want to be with people who think like they do. People who think negatively gravitate to other negative thinkers. They may not necessarily want to be around these people, but that is what happens.

Great coaches and managers always want to surround themselves with people who want to win; people who believe in themselves and their teammates can win. Who do the best athletes in individual sports train with? They choose the other top athletes. Where do the best coaches and athletes go for advice? They go to the other outstanding coaches and athletes. Who do the most ambitious people choose to associate with? I think you get the picture. Choose your peers carefully and become someone others seek out because you are a winner!

CHAPTER TWENTY-ONE·

PERFORMING IN THE CLUTCH

Many athletes never reach their potential or perform in crucial situations because they mentally succumb to the pressure. You need to train your mind to respond and to do well whether it's the bottom of the ninth inning and the score is tied or the fifth inning and your team is ahead by ten runs. Your body is the same either way. It is what is going on in your head that will make a difference.

Let's go back and talk about the scenario with the 2 x 4. If you put a 10 foot long 2 x 4 on the ground, you would be able, quite easily, to balance walk across it. Now, secure that same 2 x 4 between two buildings, 1000 feet in the air, and try walking it. The mind will dramatically change and an incredible amount of pressure and fear will overcome you even though the board and your physical self will be exactly the same. A high pressure at bat, a game changing pitch, a field goal kick that can win the game, a free throw attempt with the score tied and seconds to go, a record-setting lift. All of these situations and many others put immense mental pressure on athletes.

Some athletes come through and some do not because of their mental state. Putts are made on the 18th hole because of mental strength. All the golfers have practiced and prepared physically and, hopefully, mentally, but if the mind is not kept in a state of readiness, the body will often fail. Your mental preparation during practices must have visualized the putt dropping in the hole, the shot falling in the basket or the lift being successfully completed time after time. Whatever you planning to participate in requires mental rehearsal as well as physical preparation for success. Constantly tell yourself, "I will succeed, I will succeed, I will succeed." When the game is on the line, you have to want the ball and a chance to win the game or match. If you don't, if you hope someone other than you gets the chance, your mind is not yet ready and further practice and adjustment is required.

If you look at those athletes whom many consider to be the greatest in the clutch: Michael Jordan, Kirk Gibson, Mark Messier, George Brett, Joe Montana, Larry Bird, Magic Johnson, John Elway, Jack Nicklaus, and others, they all wanted to have the ball or the opportunity when everything was on the line. They hoped to be the one to win the game. This is the place every athlete should work towards and even strive for. This is one of the things that separate exceptional players from great ones. There are plenty of athletes with the physical talent to come through in difficult situations, but unfortunately, not as many have the mental ability to match.

Reggie Jackson was nicknamed Mr. October for good reason. He is a Baseball Hall of Famer, who hit 563 home runs in his 21-year career and was a dominating player throughout. And in the post-season he was the best. He played in five World Series with the Oakland Athletic (2) and New York Yankees (3). His overall batting average was .357 with an on base percentage of .457. He had 10 home runs and 24 RBI in 27 games. He was simply phenomenal. Jackson loved playing in crucial situations and the results showed. In the 1977 World Series with the Yankees, he set a record with 5 home runs in the series. Three of those came in the sixth- and final game. His teams won 4 of the 5 series in which he played. That is not a coincidence. When it counted, he wanted to play.

Reggie Jackson is an example of how exceptional competitors think. Even a less physically adept athlete will beat one that is superior physically if the less talented person wants it more and prepares to take charge when everything is on the line. The mind decides.

·CHAPTER TWENTY-TWO·

OVERCOMING OBSTACLES

OUT OF YOUR CONTROL

Throughout your athletic career you will encounter many obstacles that are out of your control. You must train your mind to always be prepared for this. These obstacles will be large or small and can come suddenly or with plenty of time to prepare. But, regardless of the situation you must adapt to these changes and do what you need to do to win. The obstacle may be an unexpected change in weather, a time change, wrong equipment, someone on your team not showing up, etc. But whatever the disruption you have to make adjustments and believe you will win regardless. Your mind must be trained not to give up, not to lose confidence, and to go with plan B and win with it.

You may have a huge fight, game or meet scheduled and for a reason unknown to you, your coach does not show. You don't know why you just know he or she is not there and you are on your own. What do you do? You prepare in advance to coach yourself or get the next best-available person and you do not for one minute let this change your mindset of winning. You will not physically change. You can still win! Or, the second scenario, you have a baseball game and can't find your baseball glove that fits your hand like a tailored suit fits your body. In fact, with your own glove, your hand takes on super powers and makes plays that appear to be impossible. You have used your mitt on every play you have made for two years, with only 3 errors (not the gloves fault) and now you have to use a mitt that fits poorly and with which you have never caught a baseball. Again, you must be mentally prepared and not think for a moment you won't still play your best, even with a borrowed glove.

Do not use Tombstone Courage (discussed in Chap. 4) If the scheduled game is meaningless other than as a practice game, and it won't hurt your career, you can always choose not to play if you feel sick for example. However, if you can play and will be fine, change or keep your mindset that you will win and play the game of your life. Many outstanding players have played through less than ideal conditions and done well. You get a call to take a fight in two weeks. This leaves an absolute minimum of time to train, or study your opponent, but you are going to take this fight because it is important to you. Find a way to win. Who cares if it's only two weeks? Nothing says you can't win.

Believe as strongly you can win as if you had trained six months. If you don't, your mind will weaken your body. Maybe you just lost some world class training or sparring partners and you'll have to be on your own. Don't let your mind beat you. You can still win, you can still workout and improve. Many outstanding athletes have trained in abysmal circumstances and still succeeded. Always get the best training environment available but if you can't find a way. Going back to my friend Spencer Westwood, lack of a good facility, good equipment, and good training partners never stopped him. Spencer always utilized the best gym when he could and sought out the best lifters to train with. He got the most out of whatever was available and never considered quitting.

You may also suffer a setback in the middle of a competition, but you can overcome it. If you are a coach, you really need to learn to adapt to less than ideal circumstances. In the 1980 NBA finals, going into game 6 in Philadelphia, the Los Angeles Lakers held a 3-2 advantage over the tough 76ers, led by Julius Erving. The Lakers' star center Kareem Abdul-Jabbar suffered an injury in game 5 and didn't even make the trip to Philly. Things looked bleak for L.A., but coach Paul Westhead decided to start rookie Earvin "Magic" Johnson in his place at the Center position. Many believe it was the best game of Magic's storied career. He scored 42 points had 15 rebounds, 7 assists, and 3 steals to lead the Lakers to the championship. Instead of conceding the game to the 76ers, coach Westhead improvised and had confidence in his team, and Johnson and the Lakers won. Coaching is all about mental decisions, so find a way to win. You must deal with unplanned circumstances and have confidence in yourself and in your players. Look for a way to win. Find a way to win. Never even consider losing, or that is what you will get.

·CHAPTER TWENTY-THREE·

ELEVATE YOUR IMMEDIATE

PERFORMANCE

M any times in competition you will need an extra burst of energy or a quick dose of adrenaline to make the difference between winning and losing. If you are involved in a sport which requires a short time period such as the shot put, power or Olympic lifting, arm wrestling etc., you can elevate your performance through your mind. If you are in an extended match or competition such as track, basketball, soccer, etc. and you need an extra burst of energy to provide stamina and run faster and longer at an opportune time, you need your mind to work for you.

An example is doing the bench press. The execution will only be between 5 and 20 seconds give or take. You need to give it everything you have in that short period. I always remember a WABDL meet in which I competed in 2004. Gus Restwich, a legendary powerlifter who once deadlifted 865 pounds and competed in the World's Strongest Man in the 1970's with Bill Kazmier talking about having attitude. He said you have to have an attitude, you have to bring out something from within, the monster within of aggression and you can lift an extra 20 maybe even 40 pounds. Two lifters I worked out with for years, Tommy Ponzio and Robert (Butch) Bills would lift more weight because they u s e so much adrenalin and craziness when they go under the bar. It was more than just an unexcelled effort; they harnessed something within themselves to give them more strength.

You have to train your mind to be angry and aggressive. Controlled anger and aggression for your sport is often essential on the platform, which is the only place it should be visible. You are an animal on the field but a gentleman or a lady off it. Joe Clifford was my mentor and trainer. He deadlifted 815 pounds weighing around 265. He always stressed this. He was as nice a man as you would ever meet, but he knew that showing anger and aggression would make the difference between winning and finishing second. Before Joe lifted he would be in a corner by himself, oblivious to everything around him. He was getting deep in his mind, preparing himself to reach a new level of performance, of aggression for his lift. The lift would take less than thirty seconds to complete so he knew everything had to come out for that short time. You should be able to reach a euphoric rush of adrenaline because your mind is so consumed with the task in hand. Practicing makes it happen.

At the high level of sports competition, you must gain an edge. If it is five pounds of strength or 1/10th of a second of speed, it may be the difference. Grandmothers have lifted cars off children to save them. The mind told them they had to do it. You may be fatigued but if a shark was in the water and you were ten feet from safety I guarantee you would find some energy to get away from that shark.

Joe Clifford told me practice getting mad before a lift. Think of something that would make me more aggressive. You have to think what will give you the energy. You must save your family or a child or whatever situation you can relate to where you need adrenaline. You need that same aggressiveness right now! You are in a wrestling match; it is tied, thirty seconds to go. You need that energy and adrenalin right now! Put something in your head! Get aggressive! If you were trying to get away from a Lion, you would be full of adrenalin. Think that thought. What if you were in your house with your family and someone broke in and wanted to kill you, your spouse and your children and was not going to stop. You would have only one choice to handle the situation and you would have to defend your family with everything you had.

Sports are not life or death, but you need a mentality that you will do what you need to do to win. You will not surrender. You will beat your opponent because you may not get another chance. After the match, shake hands and be a gentleman, but now is the moment you have to survive and you will pull something from deep within you to be victorious. The mind will get you there. Prepare to control your mind for this moment and then use it. Without this ability, you may give it a good effort, just as before, but that may not be enough. Go to another level.

·CHAPTER TWENTYFOUR·

BE MENTALLY PREPARED

FOR SITUATIONS

This chapter is extremely important to understand. It is closely related to Chapter 19 on Distractions and Chapter 22 on Overcoming Overwhelming Obstacles, but is not the same. You must be mentally prepared for all situations, not just things that happen out of your control and distractions that will contribute to poor performance if you do not overcome them. Of course, you must prepare for those situations and that is why there are chapters addressing them specifically. You must also mentally prepare for situations that will likely arise. A plethora of situations can occur and you must play the "what if game" before they happen. Consider the following scenarios.

You are playing centerfield. There are runners on first and second. What do you do if a fly ball comes to you deep in the outfield? What will you do if a single is hit to you? How many outs are there? Are the base-runners lightning fast or slow as molasses? Do you have a strong, accurate arm and can you throw directly to a baseman or would it be better to throw to the cutoff man? Every time you compete or practice map out in your mind what to do in every situation.

You are the quarterback, the play called is not going to work, the receivers are covered and throwing the ball is too risky. Have you done "what if?" already in your mind? What are your options now? A good coach and a good player think constantly and practice how to react to such situations. Know your sport and know your opponents so you can visualize what to do in every situation you can imagine. If you don't you may end up throwing that ball from the outfield to the wrong infielder and the opponent scores or takes additional bases on your throwing error most likely caused by lack of proper preparation.

Bill Buckner was an outstanding baseball player. Because of injuries, he played through great pain throughout much of his career. Yet he accumulated over 2700 hits and helped several of his teams reach the World Series. Unfortunately, he is primarily and unfairly remembered for a costly error he made near the end of game six of the 1986 World Series, playing for the Boston Red Sox. The New York Mets ended up winning game 6 and 7 and the Series. He was at the stage of his career when he had severe knee injuries and was often taken out late in games and replaced by Dave Stapleton, who had better defensive skills. Manager John Mcnamara did not replace Buckner in this game, as was his strategy in past games, and now we can only wonder how the game may have turned out without Buckner's error. One thing is for sure, if Mcnamara could do it over he would have replaced Buckner.

Many games and competitions have been won and lost because competitors and coaches have or have not said to themselves "what if?" You always have to be thinking about what might happen and then prepare for it.

Kirk Gibson, playing for the LA Dodgers, hit one of the most dramatic home runs in baseball history off the Oakland Athletics' star closing pitcher, Dennis Eckersley, in game one of the 1988 World Series. This did not happen by accident or luck. Gibson had been hurt and could barely walk to the plate when Los Angeles Dodger manager Tommy Lasorda put him in to pinch-hit in the ninth inning. There were two outs and a runner on base. It seemed like attempted suicide on the part of Lasorda. Gibson almost fell over on his first swing. The count went to three balls and two strikes. Gibson remembered that Mel Didier, one of the Dodgers scouts, who had been involved in baseball for fifty years and had studied Eckersley told him "Partner, as sure as I am standing, Eckersley throws a backdoor slider on a 3-2 count." Gibson planned on that and miraculously hit the ball out of the park.

It was a miracle, but that kind of miracle doesn't happen by accident. Gibson had mentally prepared and it paid off. Winning is not done by luck.

·CHAPTER TWENTY-FIVE·

TAKE A CHANCE

One of the biggest mental obstacles I have seen in people is the unwillingness to take a chance and to compete. There are many reasons for this: fear of embarrassment, feelings of inadequacy, being unprepared, lack of confidence, fear of embarrassment etc. These people will usually not admit their reasons. They are legitimate and must be overcome mentally. Many potentially excellent athletes have never competed because of these fears and you must change your mindset and take a chance to overcome these fears and reach your goals. You won't always succeed when you take a chance, but you will never succeed if you don't.

Michael Jordan left the game of basketball at the pinnacle of his career. He had just won another NBA title and was considered the greatest player in the game. But Jordan wanted to chase his dream of baseball. Many people thought he was crazy. Why would anyone take a chance to play another sport when they are so overpowering, so popular, and so successful at the one they are currently playing? Michael Jordan had something in him very few people have. He had to give baseball a chance. He didn't care what other people thought, he wanted to prove something to himself. He knew it was a risk, but he didn't want to wonder the rest of his life what might have been. He did not achieve greatness in baseball, but his fearless attitude of taking chances is what made him the Basketball Hall of Famer he is. Jordan was criticized by some for attempting another sport, but he is the rare individual that would not pass it by. He knew from years ago that without risk there is no reward.

Sugar Ray Leonard made what was called an ill-advised comeback to fight Marvin Hagler after many inactive years in retirement. Leonard had not fought in almost three years and had fought only once in five years. He would also be moving up to fight in the middleweight division, a full weight class up from welterweight where he had been a champion. Hagler had not lost a fight in eleven years and was considered the best pound for pound fighter in the world. He had beaten outstanding fighters and Hall of Famers including Thomas Hearns and Roberto Duran, who to that time was the only fighter who had ever beaten Leonard. It was a huge risk for Leonard, but he wanted to know. He was willing to take a chance. Like Jordan, this attitude made him the boxing legend he became. Playing things safe just was not the way he did things. He defeated Hagler in a close decision in one of the biggest upsets in sports history. Later Leonard lost in comeback bouts at an advanced age, but he still had the courage to take a chance. Great people take chances while other people wonder what might have been. Take a chance! That is what life is all about.

Wayne Gretzky is arguably the greatest athletes who ever lived. He completely dominated the sport of hockey while he was playing. He is widely considered the greatest hockey player of all time. He scored more goals and made more assists in his career than any player ever in the NHL. Gretzky famously said, "You miss 100% of the shots you don't take." This is a simple but perfectly accurate statement. You also don't get many opportunities to do it over in life, so do it when you can.

There is a memorable quotation by U. S. President, Theodore Roosevelt. It's an excerpt from the speech, *"Citizenship In A Republic"* delivered at the Sorbonne in Paris, on April 23, 1910: "It is not the critic who counts; not the man who points out how the strong man stumbles, or where the doer of deeds could have done them better. The credit belongs to the man who is actually in the arena, whose face is marred by dust and sweat and blood; who strives valiantly; who errs, and comes short again and again, because there is no effort without error and shortcoming; but who does actually strive to do the deeds; who knows great enthusiasms, the great devotions; who spends himself in a worthy cause; who at the best knows in the end the triumph of high achievement, and who at the worst, if he fails, at least fails while daring greatly, so that his place shall never be with those cold and timid souls who neither know victory nor defeat." Life is short. Take every opportunity you have to be somebody; whether it's trying out for the high school football team or competing in the Olympics, you must seek high achievement.

Don't let opportunity pass you by. Can you think of someone you believe had the talent to achieve great things but just didn't tryout? He or she would not sign up or take a risk? When you take a chance, there is usually nothing to lose, but everything to gain. The world is full of winners. We are all winners. We all have something in us that can do great things. There is room for everyone to be great. Take a chance!

·CHAPTER TWENTY-SIX·

SEEK THE BEST HELP

This chapter is closely related to the chapters Feeding Your Mind and Associate With Winners. In order to get benefit the most from your abilities, you need to get the best help possible through coaching, mentoring, research, reading and working with the best people available. These things will enhance your abilities and stimulate your psyche to excel, rather than just succeed. You must always be receptive and take in everything you can that may help, from any source available. Never think you have progressed so far you no longer need to listen to certain people. Your neighbor or your wise grandfather may have something to offer you. Make it a priority to seek counsel, and then carefully select that which is best for your situation.

Many powerlifters will relocate to a different state to take advantage of the things offered there. Many move to Ohio to work out with Louie Simmons and the Westside Barbell Club. Spencer Westwood travels for hours to train at Jeremy Horns Elite Performance in West Jordan Utah. Some of the best powerlifters in the world train there and the trip is worth the time and expense. Elite Performance is also home to some of the best MMA fighters on the planet. Matt Hughes, as mentioned in the chapter on Overcoming

Fear, traveled across the country to train with Jeremy Horn of Elite Performance. He needed professional training for world title fights, and he knew the training he received from Jeremy was as skilled as any in the business.

Amir Killah travelled from Michigan to Utah to train for fights and Jake Heun travelled there and literally lived in the gym, sleeping on a couch in a back room, so he could train there. To reach another level you need to feed your mind with the best knowledge and training you can find. If it means moving, make the sacrifice. If you are not able to relocate, get the absolute best help you can where you are. You must also seek the best information available through reading and studying. Read about the best training methods for your sport. There is a wealth of information available today, and much of it can be accessed without ever leaving your home.

When you train with top people, you get top results. Question others about training, dieting, sleeping, anything that will help you. Always look to the top people for help. Many athletes do not achieve their goals because they don't have the best help possible. Talk about what will make you better. Ask questions. One of the most impressive things to a coach or mentor is someone who asks questions. Have a desire to learn and improve.

In conclusion, remember, when you seek out the best help, you need to look to yourself. You will decide your future. You are responsible for your success! If you want to excel, you must do it because no one else can do it for you. You control your destiny and God wants you to succeed. Get your head in the game!

ABOUT THE AUTHOR

Lance Davis is a world class powerlifter. He has set numerous

state, national and world records in his division in numerous

federations.

He is also a sports and clinical hypnotherapist who

has worked with world class athletes.

Some of Lance's clients include

MMA legend Jeremy Horn,

Jake Heun, Amir Killah and Dave Castillo.

Lance trains in West Jordan Utah with Brutal

Powerlifting at Jeremy Horn's Elite Performance.

www.ingramcontent.com/pod-product-compliance
Lightning Source LLC
Chambersburg PA
CBHW021432180326
41458CB00001B/240